INTRODU

Choosing a name for your baby is an exciting and important decision. It's a name that your child will carry with them for the rest of their life, so it's important to choose one that you and your child will be happy with

In "The Ultimate Guide to Choosing the Perfect Baby Name," you will find helpful tips and advice on how to choose a name for your baby. The book covers various aspects of baby naming, such as popular naming trends,cultural and religious naming traditions, and tips for avoiding common naming pitfalls.

In addition, the book includes a comprehensive list of baby names, sorted by gender and origin, to help you find inspiration and ideas. Whether you're looking for a traditional name or something more unique, there's something for everyone in this list.

Ultimately, the perfect baby name is one that you and your partner both love and that fits your child's personality and character. With the help of this book, you'll be able to find the ideal name that will make your child stand out and be proud of their identity.

10 EXPERT TIPS TO CHOOSING A BABY NAME

Choosing a baby name can be an exciting but also challenging task for new parents. Here are 10 expert tips to help you select the perfect name for your little one:

1-Consider the meaning: Think about the meaning behind the name you are considering. Does it align with your values or represent something significant to you?

2-Check the popularity: You may want to avoid names that are too common or too unusual. Check popularity charts to see if your favorite names are trending.

3-Consider the sound: How does the name sound when you say it out loud? Will it be easy for others to pronounce or spell?

4-Consider family traditions: Is there a family name that you want to honor or continue? Do you have a naming tradition that you want to follow?

5-Look at the initials: Make sure the initials of the name you choose don't spell anything embarrassing or offensive.

6-Think about nicknames: Think about possible nicknames that could come from the name you choose. Do you like them? Would you be okay if your child is called by a different name?

7-Check for meanings in other languages: Make sure the name doesn't have any negative connotations in other languages or cultures.

8-Think about the future: Will the name still be appropriate and relevant when your child is an adult? Avoid names that are too trendy or may be difficult to pronounce.

9-Try saying it with the surname: Make sure the name you choose goes well with your surname. Test it out by saying the full name aloud.

10-Trust your instincts: Ultimately, the name you choose should feel right to you and your partner. Don't be afraid to go with your gut feeling.

Contents

Top 100 Baby Boy Names

ALEXANDER Means: Defender of Man Origin: Greek	**AIDEN** Means: Fiery One Origin: Irish	**ANTHONY** Means: Priceless One Origin: Latin
ANDREW Means: Manly, Brave Origin: Greek	**AARON** Means: Lofty, Inspired Origin: Hebrew	**ADRIAN** Means: Dark Origin: German
ANGEL Means: Messenger From God Origin: Latin	**AUSTIN** Means: Great One, Magnificent Origin: Latin	**ADAM** Means: Son of the Red Earth Origin: Hebrew
ASHER Means: Happiness Origin: Hebrew	**BENJAMIN** Means: Treasured Son Origin: Hebrew	**BRAYDEN** Means: Broad Hillside Origin: English

Top 100 Baby Boy Names

BRANDON
Means:
From the Beacon Hill
Origin:
English

BENTLEY
Means:
Meadow With Bent Grass
Origin:
English

BLAKE
Means:
Dark or Light
Origin:
Scottish

BRODY
Means:
Fortification, Castle
Origin:
Scottish

BRYSON
Means:
Noble's Son
Origin:
English

CHRISTOPHER
Means:
One Who Carries Christ
Origin:
Greek

CARTER
Means:
Cart Driver
Origin:
English

CALEB
Means:
Abundance
Origin:
Biblical

CHRISTIAN
Means:
Follower of Christ
Origin:
Greek

CHARLES
Means:
Manly
Origin:
French

CONNOR
Means:
Strong Willed, Wise
Origin:
Irish

CAMERON
Means:
Crooked Nose
Origin:
Celtic

Top 100 Baby Boy Names

COLTON
Means:
From the Dark Town
Origin:
English

CHASE
Means:
Huntsman
Origin:
English

COOPER
Means:
Barrel Maker
Origin:
English

CARSON
Means:
Why?
Origin:
Scottish/Gaelic

DANIEL
Means:
Noble's Son
Origin:
English

DYLAN
Means:
Influence
Origin:
Welsh

DAVID
Means:
Beloved
Origin:
Hebrew

DOMINIC
Means:
Lord
Origin:
Latin

EASTON
Means:
From East Town
Origin:
English

ELI
Means:
Defender of People
Origin:
Greek

ELIJAH
Means:
God Is Strong
Origin:
Hebrew

ETHAN
Means:
Strong, Valiant
Origin:
Hebrew

Top 100 Baby Boy Names

GABRIEL
Means:
God Is My Strength
Origin:
Hebrew

GAVIN
Means:
White Hawk
Origin:
Scottish

GRAYSON
Means:
Son of a Steward
Origin:
English

HENRY
Means:
Rules the Home
Origin:
French

HUNTER
Means:
Hunter
Origin:
English

HUDSON
Means:
Hardy, Strong
Origin:
English

ISAAC
Means:
Laughs, Rejoices
Origin:
Hebrew

ISAIAH
Means:
The Salvation of the Lord
Origin:
Hebrew

IAN
Means:
God Is Gracious
Origin:
Scottish

JACOB
Means:
Replacement
Origin:
Hebrew

JAMES
Means:
Replacement
Origin:
Hebrew

JAYDEN
Means:
Healer
Origin:
English

Top 100 Baby Boy Names

JOSEPH
Means:
May God Give Increase
Origin:
Hebrew

JACKSON
Means:
God Is Gracious
Origin:
Polish

JOSHUA
Means:
The Lord Is My Salvation
Origin:
Hebrew

JOHN
Means:
Gift From God
Origin:
Hebrew

JONATHAN
Means:
Gift From God
Origin:
Hebrew

JACK
Means:
God Is Gracious
Origin:
Polish

JULIAN
Means:
Youthful
Origin:
French

JEREMIAH
Means:
Exalt the Lord
Origin:
Hebrew

JORDAN
Means:
Flowing Downward
Origin:
Hebrew

JAXON
Means:
God Is Gracious
Origin:
Polish

JOSIAH
Means:
The Lord Supports
Origin:
Hebrew

JUSTIN
Means:
Just, Righteous
Origin:
Latin

Top 100 Baby Boy Names

JACE
Means:
Healing
Origin:
Greek

JAXSON
Means:
God Is Gracious
Origin:
Polish

JUAN
Means:
Gift From God
Origin:
Hebrew

KEVIN
Means:
Gentle
Origin:
Celtic

KAYDEN
Means:
Fiery One
Origin:
Irish

LIAM
Means:
Resolute Protector
Origin:
Irish

LOGAN
Means:
Servant
Origin:
Scottish

LUCAS
Means:
Light
Origin:
French

LUKE
Means:
Light
Origin:
Latin

LANDON
Means:
From the Long Hill
Origin:
English

LEVI
Means:
Joined, Attached
Origin:
Hebrew

LINCOLN
Means:
Lake, Pool
Origin:
Celtic

Top 100 Baby Boy Names

LUIS
Means:
Famous Warrior
Origin:
German

MASON
Means:
Stone Worker
Origin:
English

MICHAEL
Means:
Gift From God
Origin:
Hebrew

MATTHEW
Means:
Gift of God
Origin:
Hebrew

MATEO
Means:
God's Gift
Origin:
Spanish

NOAH
Means:
Rest, Comfort
Origin:
Hebrew

NATHAN
Means:
Gift From God
Origin:
Hebrew

NICHOLAS
Means:
Victorious
Origin:
Spanish

NOLAN
Means:
Noble
Origin:
Celtic

NATHANIEL
Means:
Gift of God
Origin:
Hebrew

OWEN
Means:
Young Warrior
Origin:
Welsh

OLIVER
Means:
Affectionate
Origin:
Norse

Top 100 Baby Boy Names

PARKER

Means:

Keeper of the Forest

Origin:

English

RYAN

Means:

Little King

Origin:

Gaelic

ROBERT

Means:

Bright With Fame

Origin:

English

SAMUEL

Means:

Told by God

Origin:

Hebrew

SEBASTIAN

Means:

Revered, Adored

Origin:

Greek

THOMAS

Means:

Twin

Origin:

Greek

TYLER

Means:

Tile Maker

Origin:

French

TRISTAN

Means:

A Knight

Origin:

Latin

Uilliam

Means:

Resolute defender

Origin:

German and English

Uriel

Means:

Angel of light

Origin:

Hebrew

Vardan

Means:

from the green hill

Origin:

French

Vernon

Means:

Alder tree or grove

Origin:

English

Top 100 Baby Boy Names

Walker

Means:

fuller of cloth

Origin:

English and German

Warren

Means:

protector and loyal

Origin:

English and German

XAVIER

Means:

Bright, Splendid

Origin:

Spanish

Yael

Means:

to ascend

Origin:

Hebrew

ZACHARY

Means:

Remembered by God

Origin:

Hebrew

Top 100 Baby Girl Names

AVA
Means:
Living One
Origin:
German

ABIGAIL
Means:
My Father's Joy
Origin:
Hebrew

AMELIA
Means:
Industrious
Origin:
Latin

AVERY
Means:
Counselor
Origin:
French

ADDISON
Means:
Battle Mighty
Origin:
English

ANNA
Means:
Gracious Favor
Origin:
Hebrew

AUDREY
Means:
Noble Strength
Origin:
English

ALLISON
Means:
Noble
Origin:
German and French

ALEXIS
Means:
Defender of Mankind
Origin:
Greek

ALEXA
Means:
Protector of Mankind
Origin:
Greek

ALYSSA
Means:
Noble
Origin:
French, German

ARIANA
Means:
Very Holy One
Origin:
Greek

Top 100 Baby Girl Names

ASHLEY
Means:
Lives in the Ash
Tree Groves
Origin:
English

Autumn
Means:
Autumn
Origin:
English

ALEXANDRA
Means:
Defender of Mankind
Origin:
Greek

ANNABELLE
Means:
Grace
Origin:
Hebrew, Latin

BELLA
Means:
Beautiful
Origin:
Latin

BRIANNA
Means:
Strong One
Origin:
Celtic-Gaelic

BROOKLYN
Means:
Broken Land
Origin:
Dutch

BAILEY
Means:
Steward
Origin:
English

CHARLOTTE
Means:
Little and Womanly
Origin:
English

CHLOE
Means:
Blooming
Origin:
Greek

CHARLOTTE
Means:
Little and Womanly
Origin:
English

CAMILA
Means:
Attendant
Origin:
Latin

Top 100 Baby Girl Names

CLAIRE
Means:
Clear and Bright
Origin:
Latin

CAROLINE
Means:
Free Person
Origin:
German and French

Davina
Means:
beloved
Origin:
Scottish/Hebrew

Delphine
Means:
dolphin
Origin:
French

Dominique
Means:
'of the Lord'
Origin:
French

Daphne
Means:
laurel or bay tree
Origin:
Greek

Daria
Means:
upholder of the good
Origin:
Greek

Decima
Means:
tenth
Origin:
Latin

ELIZABETH
Means:
Consecrated to God
Origin:
English

EMMA
Means:
Whole, Complete
Origin:
Latin

EMILY
Means:
Industrious
Origin:
Latin

EVELYN
Means:
Life
Origin:
Hebrew

Top 100 Baby Girl Names

ELLA
Means:
Illumination
Origin:
Greek

Fiadh
Means:
wild
Origin:
Irish

Fallon
Means:
leader
Origin:
Irish

Fiona
Means:
white, fair
Origin:
Gaelic

Fayola
Means:
'walks with honour'
Origin:
Yoruba

Githa
Means:
war
Origin:
Old Norse

Gloria
Means:
glory
Origin:
Latin

Greta
Means:
pearl
Origin:
German

Heledd
Means:
pool of salt
Origin:
Welsh

Helen
Means:
bright, shining light
Origin:
Greek

Henrietta
Means:
estate ruler
Origin:
French

Hilary
Means:
cheerful
Origin:
Latin

Top 100 Baby Girl Names

Ida
Means:
hard-working
Origin:
German

Isabella
Means:
'God's promise'
Origin:
Hebrew

Imelda
Means:
all-consuming fight
Origin:
Italian

Ivana
Means:
'God is gracious'
Origin:
Slavic

Jada
Means:
good and beautiful woman
Origin:
Hebrew/Arabic

Janette
Means:
gift from God
Origin:
Hebrew

Jayla
Means:
victory
Origin:
American/Hebrew

Joni
Means:
'God is gracious'
Origin:
Hebrew

kristin
Means:
'follower of Christin'
Origin:
Scottish

Kirstin
Means:
'follower of Christ'
Origin:
Scottish

Kyla
Means:
narrow spit of land
Origin:
Celtic

Lyla
Means:
night
Origin:
Arabic

Top 100 Baby Girl Names

Lyra
Means:
a lyre, small harp
Origin:
Greek

Marjorie
Means:
pearl
Origin:
Scottish

Morag
Means:
great
Origin:
Scottish

Niamh
Means:
bright
Origin:
Irish

Nola
Means:
white-shouldered
Origin:
Irish

Nora
Means:
light
Origin:
Irish

Nuala
Means:
fair-shouldered
Origin:
Irish

Opal
Means:
gem, precious
Origin:
Sanskrit

Penny
Means:
weaver
Origin:
English

Polly
Means:
star of the sea
Origin:
English

Pippa
Means:
lover of horses
Origin:
Greek

Querida
Means:
well loved
Origin:
Spanish

Top 100 Baby Girl Names

RILEY	RUBY	Rae
Means:	Means:	Means:
Little Stream	Red Jewel	ewe
Origin:	Origin:	Origin:
English	English	Hebrew

Rita	Ruth	SOPHIA
Means:	Means:	Means:
pearl	compassionate friend	Wise
Origin:	Origin:	Origin:
Spanish	Hebrew	Greek

SOFIA	SAMANTHA	SCARLETT
Means:	Means:	Means:
Wisdom	Listens Well to God	Red
Origin:	Origin:	Origin:
Greek	Aramaic	English

SAVANNAH	Tina	Tracy
Means:	Means:	Means:
From the Open Plain	river	brave
Origin:	Origin:	Origin:
Spanish	English	English

Top 100 Baby Girl Names

Trishelle
Means:
noble
Origin:
English

Tinsley
Means:
'Tynni's meadow'
Origin:
English

Ualani
Means:
heavenly rain
Origin:
Hawaiian

Ursula
Means:
little bear
Origin:
Latin

Vanessa
Means:
butterfly
Origin:
English

Valentina
Means:
strong,healthy
Origin:
Latin

Vittoria
Means:
victory
Origin:
Italian

Venetia
Means:
blessed
Origin:
Celtic

Veronica
Means:
truth
Origin:
Greek

Winter
Means:
winter
Origin:
English

Westlyn
Means:
river
Origin:
English

Whitney
Means:
brave
Origin:
English

Top 100 Baby Girl Names

Yua

Means:

blinding love

Origin:

Japanese

Yolanda

Means:

violet flower

Origin:

Greek

ZOEY

Means:

Life

Origin:

Greek

ZOE

Means:

Life

Origin:

Greek

UNISEX NAMES THAT WORK FOR BOYS AND GIRLS

NAME	OROGIN AND MEANS
Abalone	is a unique baby name of Welsh origin meaning 'bird'
Ace	this English baby name can mean 'unity' or 'noble' but is most often used to describe someone who excels
Adair	is a strong name of Old German origin meaning 'wealthy spear'
Addison	this badass unisex name means son of Adam and is of Old English
Aderyn	is a unique baby name of Welsh origin meaning 'bird'
Adrian	is a cute name of Latin and Greek origin meaning 'son of Adria'
Aiden	is a cute baby name of Irish origin and means "fiery one". Perfect for a rambunctious little bundle of joy!
Ainsley	this uncommon non binary baby name means 'meadow' and is of Gaelic origin
Alaska	is a unique name of Native American origin meaning 'great land' or 'mainland'
Alex	this name is quite a popular choice for boys and girls and means 'defender' or 'protector of humanity' and is of Greek origin
Altair	is a cool name of Arabic origin meaning 'bird, falcon'
Amari	can mean 'eternal' (Hebrew origin) or 'strength' (African origin)
Amaris	is a beautiful name of Hebrew origin meaning 'promised by God'
Andy	is an English baby name with Greek roots meaning 'brave, manly'
Angel	is such a sweet name for your bundle of joy that means 'messenger of God' and is of Greek origin
Aquarius	is a unique name of Latin origin meaning 'water bearer'

NAME	OROGIN AND MEANS
Arbor	is a cute nature-inspired cool nonbinary name that refers to the 'arbor tree' and is of English origin
Archer	I love this strong and beautiful English unisex baby name that means 'one who wields a bow and arrow'
Arden	is a Hebrew name that means 'a place of great beauty and solitude'
Ari	this super cute name is suitable for a boy or girl and means 'superior' and is of Greek origin
Arien	is a unique nonbinary name of Hebrew origin meaning 'enchanted' or 'most pure' (Greek origin)
Aries	is a cute astrology inspired name of Latin origin meaning 'the ram'
Ariel	this was primarily a boy name that became quite popular for girls after The Little Mermaid- and it means 'lion of God' and is of Hebrew origin
Arlan	is a Gaelic baby name meaning 'pledge' or 'oath'
Arlo	has kind of a hipster vibe. It is of Old English origin and means 'rock hill' or 'fortified hill'
Armani	is a cute name of Italian origin meaning 'warrior'
Arrow	if you want a boho gender-neutral name, this one is pretty cute! This English name means 'A Projectile Fired From A Bow'
Asher	this adorable baby name is of Hebrew origin and means 'happy' or 'blessed'
Ashlen	is a cute English name meaning 'meadow of ash trees'
Astin	this pretty unique gender neutral name is of French origin and means 'starlike'
Ashton	this beautiful name means "ash tree town" and is of English origin
Aspen	this oh so boho baby name comes from Aspen trees and means 'quaking trees' and is of American origin
Aster	is a gender-neutral name of Greek origin meaning 'star' or it can refer to the flower of the same name
Atlas	is a baby name of Greek origin meaning 'bearer of the heavens' or 'to carry'

NAME	OROGIN AND MEANS
Aubrey	is a cute name of German and French origin meaning 'ruler of elves'
Audin/Audyn	this Egnlish baby name means 'old friend' or 'half Danish
August	is another one of those hippie baby names and is of Latin origin. It means 'exalted'
Austen	this lovely gender neutral baby name means 'great and magnificent and is of Latin origin
Averill	is an Old English name meaning 'boar battle'
Avery	is a beautiful baby name of English and French origin meaning 'ruler of elves'
Azariah	is a unique Hebrew baby name meaning 'helped by God'
Bailey	this is an Old English occupational name from Medieval times meaning 'bailiff'
Baker	is an English occupational name meaning 'baker'
Banks	is an English baby name meaning 'one who lives on the hillside or riverbank'
Basil	is a cute plant inspired name of Greek origin meaning 'royal, kingly'
Bay	this short and cute gender neutral French baby name means 'auburn haired'
Baylor	is an uncommon name of English origin meaning 'delivery person'
Bear	is a cute bohemian animal inspired choice of German origin meaning 'strong and brave as a bear'
Beck	this cute name means 'one living beside a small stream' and is of Old Norse origin
Beckett	another super cute unisex baby name and this one means bee cottage
Bellamy	is an uncommon baby name of French and Irish origin meaning 'good friend' or 'handsome friend'
Bentley	although we associate it with the car of the same name these days, this Old English baby name actually means 'a clearing covered with bent grass'

NAME	OROGIN AND MEANS
Berkley	is a name of Old English and Scottish origin meaning 'birch tree meadow'
Birch	is a cute Old English name meaning 'shining, bright' or 'birch tree'
Blair	comes from Gaelic dialect and means 'plains' or 'fields' traditionally a boy name but has become very popular with girls
Blaise	this lovely name is of French and Latin origin and means 'lisp' or 'stutter'
Blake	another popular boy name that has become a favorite for girls and means 'dark and attractive'
Blaze	this cool English name means 'fire'
Bliss	this cute and unique English name means 'perfect joy' or 'intense happiness'
Bobby	is a rare nonbinary name of Indian origin meaning 'awakening' or 'enlightenment'
Bowie	is a cute gender neutral name of Scottish origin meaning 'blond'
Braden	is an English baby name meaning 'broad valley, 'broad hillside', or 'salmon'
Brady	is an Irish name meaning 'broad meadow', 'spirited', or 'descendant of Bradach'
Brecken	is an uncommon name of Irish origin meaning 'freckled' or 'descended from Breacan'
Brenner	is of Old German origin and means 'to burn'
Brennon	this name has Irish origins and means 'prince' or 'teardrop'
Brett	is a Celtic baby name meaning 'of Brittany'
Brooklyn	is a beautiful English name meaning 'beautiful brook'
Briar	this unique nonbinary name is of English origin and means 'thorny bush of wild roses'
Briley	is a cute gender-neutral name of Irish origin meaning 'descendant of Roghallach' or 'woodland, meadow', 'briar wood'

NAME	OROGIN AND MEANS
Caelan	this beautiful Irish name seems to have a few different meanings including: 'slender, narrow or fine', 'strong warrior' or 'people of victory'
Callahan	this name has Irish origins and has some vague meanings but the most common are 'lovers of church' or 'bright headed'
Callaway	this cute and uncommon English name means 'pebbly place'
Callen	this strong unique baby name means 'powerful in battle'
Camden	is a name of Scottish origin meaning 'winding valley'
Cameron	is a Gaelic baby name meaning 'crooked nose' or 'bent nose'
Campbell	this cute name is of Scottish origin and means 'from the beautiful field'
Camren	this Spanish name means 'garden' and makes a great addition to your nonbinary names list
Carden	this occupational Old English name means 'wood carder'
Carey	this feminine name can be used for boys and girls and means 'from the fort' (Welsh origin) or 'love' (Irish origin)
Carlin	this adorable and unique baby name has Irish origins and means 'little champion'
Caron	is a name of Welsh origin meaning 'to love, kindhearted' or 'pure' (Greek origin)
Carrigan	this uncommon name of Irish origin means 'pointed' or 'spear'
Carson	is a name of Scandinavian origin meaning 'son of marsh dwellers'
Carter	is a cute English occupational name meaning 'driver of a cart'
Casey	this Gaelic baby name is another great nonbinary name and means 'vigilant' or 'watchful'
Cassidy	this cute Irish name means 'clever' or 'curly haired'
Cedar	is a cute nature baby name for boys or girls inspired by trees and eans 'cedar tree' (Egnlish origin)

NAME	OROGIN AND MEANS
Channing	this gender-neutral name can mean 'wise' or 'young wolf' and is of English and Old French origin
Charlie	this classic unisex baby name is oh so cute and means 'free man' and is of English origin
Clarke	is a baby name of Latin origin meaning 'cleric' or 'clerk' and makes a great masculine girl name or boy name
Cody	this one can mean a 'helpful person' or 'son of Odo (wealthy)' and is an English name
Corey	this cute name means 'from the round hill', 'heart', 'maiden', 'multitude' or 'raven' and is of Irish origin
Corwin	is a cool Gaelic and Old English name meaning 'from beyond the hill' or 'heart's friend, companion'
Cove	is a unique nonbinary name of English origin meaning 'small bay' or 'small coastal inlet'
Cruise	is a unisex badass name of English origin meaning 'bold, fierce'
Crosby	is a unique name of Scandinavian origin meaning 'at the cross'
Dallas	this is a place name and means 'from Dallas' (Scotland), 'from the dalles', or 'the valley meadows' and is of Scottish origin
Dakota	this super cute and unique unisex name means 'friends' or 'friendly' and is of Native American origin
Dana	is a classic English name of Hebrew origin meaning 'God has judged'
Danner	is a baby name of German origin meaning 'dweller near the fig tree' or 'people of the forest'
Darcy	this vintage unisex name has a few different meanings including 'dark one' or 'from the fortress' and is of Irish origin
Dawson	this was an English medieval nickname and means 'son of David'
Dean	this English name also has multiple meanings depending on what origin you look at but the most common are 'monk', 'dignitary' or 'valley'
Demi	is a short and cute unisex name of French origin meaning 'half'
Denim	is an unusual baby name of French origin meaning 'strong cloth'

NAME	OROGIN AND MEANS
Denver	comes from Old English and French and means 'green valley'
Devan	I love this badass unisex name! It means 'divine'. How perfect! It is of Frech origin.
Dion	is a short name of Greek origin meaning 'god of wine'
Dominique	is a long name of French and Latin origin meaning 'lord'
Drew	this name was classically male but now is considered a masculine girl name as well and means 'strong, manly and brave' and is of Welsh origin
Dylan	another perfect name that works for boys or girls and means 'born from the sea'- how romantic!
Easton	this name means 'east facing place' and is of English origin
Eden	is a name of Hebrew origin meaning 'place of pleasure'
Eli	this Hebrew name means 'my God', 'high, elevated'
Ellery	this cute English baby name means 'joyful or happy' (or Island of elder trees)
Elliott	is a more masculine nonbinary name of Hebrew origin meaning 'the Lord is my God'
Ellis	is a baby name of Welsh origin meaning 'benevolent'
Ellison	this non binary name means 'son of Elder' and is of Old English origin
Elm	is a tree name that could work for boys or girls. It means 'red, brown' or 'one who lives near the elm tree grove and is of English origin
Ember	is a unique name of English origin meaning 'spark, low burning'
Emerson	this name means 'son of Emery' and is associated with bravery and is of Old English origin
Emery	this beautiful unisex name has German origins and means 'brave' or 'powerful'
Erin	this cute Gaelic baby name means 'from the island to the west (referring to Ireland) and 'peace'

NAME	OROGIN AND MEANS
Evan	this is a form of John in Hebrew and means ' God is gracious'
Everest	this strong gender neutral name is of English origin and means 'dweller on the Eure river'
Everette	is a cute name of Old English (with German roots) origin meaning 'brace, strong boar'
Everly	is an English name meaning 'wild boar in the woodland clearing'
Evren	is a name of Turkish origin meaning 'the universe, cosmos'
Ezra	is a cute Hebrew baby name meaning 'help' or 'helper'
Fable	is a cute modern English name meaning 'tale, story, legend'
Fallon	traditionally a surname but has become a fairly popular nonbinary first name and means 'leader' or 'grandchild of a rich king'
Farren	another surname turned first name - this one means 'adventurous' and is of English origin- love that!
Fay(e)	this short unisex name means 'confidence, trust, belief'- or add an e at the end and it means 'fairy' (Old French and English origin)
Fenix	is a unique baby name of Greek origin meaning 'dark red'
Fennec	this cute and uncommon name means 'fox' and is of Arabic origin
Fernley	is an Old English name meaning 'fern meadow'
Fig	is a short and sweet plant inspired baby name meaning 'dweller near the fig tree' and is of English origin
Finch	is a cute English name meaning 'songbird'
Finley	this adorable unisex baby name has Gaelic origins and means 'fair-haired warrior'
Floris	is a name of Latin origin meaning 'flower'
Flynn	this cute Irish name means 'reddish (complexion)'

NAME	OROGIN AND MEANS
Forrest	is a cool nature themed name meaning 'dweller near the woods' and is of English origin
Francis	comes from Latin and Italian origin and means 'free man' or 'Frenchmen'
Frankie	this name comes from France and means 'free one'- super cute for a boy or girl
Gabriel	is a Hebrew baby name meaning 'God is my strength'
Gael	this sweet unisex name means 'joyful' 'blessed, generous' (Irish) or 'my father rejoices' (Hebrew)
Gardner	is a cute and unique name from Middle English meaning 'keeper of the garden'
Garner	is a name of Middle English origin meaning 'to gather grain'
Garnet	is a jewel name of English origin meaning 'pomegranate'
Gene	is an English baby name that means 'well born'
Gentry	is a name of English origin meaning 'of gentle or good breeding
Georgie	is a cute name of Greek origin meaning 'farmer'
Gerrie	is a name that comes from Old German and means 'spear ruler'
Gianni	is an Italian name with Greek and Hebrew roots meaning 'God is gracious'
Gili	this short and cute name means 'happiness' or 'eternal joy' and is of Hebrew origin
Grayson	I love this beautiful badass unisex baby name which means 'son of the gray-haired one' and is of English origin
Greer	isn't a popular nonbinary name, it is of Scottish origin and means 'watchful' or 'vigilant'
Guadalupe	is a unique gender-neutral name of Spanish origin meaning 'river of the wolf'
Guthrie	this cute name is of Irish origin and means 'windy place'

NAME	OROGIN AND MEANS
Hadley	this English name means 'heather field"
Hale	s an Old English name meaning 'hero or dweller from the hall'
Halston	is an English baby name meaning 'holy stone'
Harbor	is a unique non binary name of English origin meaning 'protected from the storm' or 'sheltered in the calm waters'
Harlem	is a name of Dutch origin meaning 'home on the wooded hill'
Harley	this Old English name means 'hare's meadow'
Harlow	this was traditionally a surname that means 'one who lives around a rocky area' and is of English origin
Harper	a very popular unisex baby name of English origin that means 'harp player'- how cute!
Hart	is a short and cute name of English origin meaning 'bear', 'hero', or 'stag'
Haskell	is a name of Hebrew and Old Norse origin meaning 'intellect' or 'the cauldron of God'
Haven	this English name means 'safe place'
Hayden	this English name means 'from the valley'
Hayes	is an English baby name meaning 'hedged area'
Haylen	could mean 'hall of light' of 'dweller from the hall' (English origin) or 'fire' (Scottish origin)
Henley	another cute name that works for boys or girls and this one means 'high meadow' and is of English origin
Holland	is a name of Dutch origin meaning 'wooded land'
Hollis	this cute name comes from Old English and means 'from the grove of holly trees'- perfect for a winter baby
Honor	is a virtue inspired baby name of English origin meaning 'to be held in high respect or esteem'

NAME	OROGIN AND MEANS
Hudson	traditionally a surname, this one can mean 'Hugh's son' and is of English origin
Hunter	this name means just what it sounds like, 'one who hunts' and is of English origin
Hutton	is a name of Old English origin meaning 'settlement on the ridge'
Idra	is an Aramaic name of Hebrew origin meaning 'fig tree'
Idris	is a name of Welsh origin meaning 'prophet' or 'fiery leader'
Iman	this name has African origins and means 'faith'
Imani	is a name of Arabic origin meaning 'belief' or 'faith'
Indiana	is a pretty badass non binary name of English and American origin meaning 'land of the Indians' or 'from India'
Indie	this name can mean 'blue (indigo)' or 'from India' and is of American origin
Indigo	this rare unisex name is of Greek origin and means 'dye from India'
Ira	this name means 'watchful' or 'vigilant' and is of Hebrew origin
Irving	is a cute baby name of Gaelic origin meaning 'fresh or green water'
Isa	meaning 'strong-willed one' and is of German and Arabic origin
Jace	this is a Hebrew name that means 'the Lord is salvation"
Jackie	this cool unisex name means 'God is gracious' and is of English origin
Jade	is a name of Spanish origin meaning 'stone of the side'
Jae	this is traditionally a Japanese boy name that means 'talent' or 'wealth'
Jalen	this cute and unique name has Greek origins and means 'healer'

NAME	OROGIN AND MEANS
Jagger	this aesthetic nonbinary name has a little rock and roll flair (thanks to Mick Jagger), it actually means 'carter' or 'one who cuts' and is of English origin
James	this classical boy name of Hebrew origin has become more popular with girls too, it means 'supplanter'
Jamie	this classic gender neutral name has Scottish origins and means 'supplanter'
Jaycee	this cute name means 'healer' or 'moon' and is of American origin
Jayden	this adorable name is perfect for a boy or girl and means 'thankful' or 'God will judge' and is of Hebrew origin
Jaylin	is a cute name of American and Greek origin meaning 'supplanter', 'calm' or 'jaybird
Jenesis	is a rare name of Hebrew origin meaning 'origin', 'beginning' or 'birth'
Jennis	is a modern English and American name meaning 'God is gracious'
Jericho	is a cute biblical boy name of Greek and Arabic origin meaning 'city of the moon' or 'fragrant'
Jesiah	is an uncommon baby name of Hebrew origin meaning 'the Lord exists'
Jesse	this cute name works for a boy or girl and means 'gift' or 'the Lord exits' and is of Hebrew origin
Jett	sounds like a pretty cool badass unisex name, it means 'jet black' and is of English origin
Jody	this Hebrew baby name means 'Jewess', 'praised' or 'God increases' and is of Hebrew origin
Joey	this is another very popular unisex name and means 'God will increase' and is a Hebrew baby name. It is usually a nickname for Joseph or Josephine
Jordan	this name has religious origins and often refers to the River Jordan in Palestine. It means 'to flow down' or 'descend' and is of Hebrew origin
Jori	this short and cute unisex means 'down flowing' and is of Hebrew origin
Journey	is a modern invented American name meaning 'trip or experience from one place to another'
Jove	is a unique name of Latin origin meaning 'father of the sky' or 'Jupiter'

NAME	OROGIN AND MEANS
Jude	this Hebrew name means 'praise'
Jules	is a name of French origin meaning 'young'
Julian	is a has Latin and Greek roots and means 'youthful'
Juniper	is a plant inspired name of Latin origin meaning 'young' or 'bearing Juniper berries'
Justice	is an English name meaning 'just', 'upright', 'righteous'
Kaden	is a name of Arabic and American origin meaning 'fighter', 'battle', or 'champion'
Kadence	is a unique name of Latin origin meaning 'with rhythm'
Kaelin	is a Gaelic baby name that can mean: 'slender', 'fair', 'rejoicer', 'waterfall', or 'pool'
Kai	this is a favorite of mine! Kai is a Hawaiian baby name that means from the sea- many, if not most, Hawaiian baby names are gender neutral so take a look at the full list!
Kalan	this cute name means 'slender' or 'fair' and is of Gaelic origin
Kale	this plant inspired name has English and German origins and means 'free man'
Kamari	is an Arabic name meaning 'moon' or Sanskrit for 'the enemy of desire'
Kapri	is an uncommon English name meaning 'caprice'
Karel	this German baby name means 'manly' or 'free man'
Karson	is the Americanized version of a Scottish baby name meaning 'son of the marsh-dwellers' or 'free man'
Kasey	is a baby name of Irish origin meaning 'alert' or 'vigorous'
Kayra	is a cool Turkish baby name meaning 'gift of God'
Keaton	is an Old English place name meaning 'place of hawks'

NAME	OROGIN AND MEANS
Keegan	this is traditionally an Irish clan name and means 'son of fire'
Kellan	depending on what origin you look at, this intersex baby name means 'swamp' (German origin), 'slender' or ' descendent of the bright headed one' (Irish origin)
Kelly	is one of those gender neutral names that are more feminine, it is of Irish origin and means 'bright-headed'
Kelsey	is a cute Old English name meaning 'ship's victory'
Kendall	this is an Old English baby name that comes from the River Kent and means 'royal valley'
Kendry	this beautiful and unique name is of Malagasy origin and means 'wise man' or 'son of Henry' (Scottish origin)
Kennedy	this strong intersex baby name has a bit of a funny meaning 'misshapen head' or 'helmeted head' and is of Irish origin
Kerri	is a cool Gaelic baby name meaning 'dark, mysterious' or 'descendent of Ciar'
Kester	is a lovely name of Gaelic and Greek origin meaning 'carrier of Christ'
Khari	this beautiful African baby name means 'kingly' or 'born to rule'
Kian	this short and cute baby name means 'ancient' (Irish origin) or 'God is gracious' (Hebrew origin for Keon)
Kieran	this adorable Gaelic baby name means 'dark one' or 'dark-haired one'
Kiernan	is a strong name of Irish origin meaning 'black'
Kingsley	this old English name means "king's meadow"
Kit	this short and cute English name means 'bearer of Christ'
Knox	is a Scottish baby name that means 'rounded hill'
Kris	is an English name with Latin roots meaning 'follower of Christ'
Kylan	is a cute baby name of Gaelic origin meaning 'narrow or straight'

NAME	OROGIN AND MEANS
Kyler	this badass unisex baby name has Irish origins and is a place name describing 'the narrow;' a wood or a church. I like the Danish meaning which is a 'bowman' or 'archer'
Kyrie	this Gaelic unisex name meaning 'dark' is pretty cute!
Lachlan	this super cute Scottish baby name means "from the fjord-land' and was used to describe Vikings
Laken	this English baby name means 'lake' or 'pool'
Landyn	this English place name means 'from the long hill or ridge'
Landry	this cute name of French origin means 'ruler'
Lane	I stole this one from Gilmore Girls (remember Rory's BFF?) this name means 'from the long meadow/path' and is an English baby name
Langley	this English baby name means 'long meadow'
Lauren	this name has become fairly popular for those seeking a feminine boy name and means 'laurel plant' or 'wisdom' and is of French origin
Laurent	this French name has Roman and Old Greek origins and means 'the bright one' or 'the shining one'
Leaf	is a cute boho nature name of English origin and means 'dear, darling
Leighton	this English baby name means 'Herb garden-from the meadow or farm'- I've loved this name since Gossip Girl, anybody else?
Lennon	this name comes from the Gaelic term for 'lover' or 'dear one'
Lennox	this is also another Gaelic baby name and means 'with many elm trees'
Leslie	this name can mean 'the garden of hollies' (Scottish origin) or 'the gray fort' (Scottish) or 'joyful' (English origin) depending on what origin you look at
Lex	this short androgynous name is of Greek origin and means 'defender of men'
Lincoln	this one has become more popular in the unisex name category these days and means 'Roman colony at the pool' or 'a lakeside colony' and is of English origin
Linden	is a tree name of English origin meaning 'lime tree' or 'linden tree hill'

NAME	OROGIN AND MEANS
Lindsey	is another nonbinary nature name, it is of Scottish origin and means 'island of linden trees' or 'Lincoln's marsh'
Logan	this cute Scottish name means 'little hallow'
Lonnie	this German baby name means 'ready for battle'
Lynx	this unique animal inspired name is of Greek origin and means 'brightness'
Lyric	perfect for a musical family- this name comes from the phrase 'from the lyre-song' and is of Greek origin
Mackenzie	this adorable Scottish name means 'born of fire' but can also mean 'child of the wise leader'
Madison	this name means 'son of Matthew or Maude' and is of English origin
Madden	is a baby name of Irish origin meaning 'little dog' or 'puppy'
Maddox	this name can mean 'fortunate' or 'son of Madoc' and is of Welsh origin
Maitland	this name may mean 'Matthew's land' or 'meadow' and is of Old Scottish origin
Majesty	this cute royalty inspired name is of Latin origin and means 'royal bearing, dignity'
Maple	this cute plant inspired name is Enof English origin and means 'maple tree'
Marin	is a name of Latin origin meaning 'of the sea'
Marley	this English name means 'pleasant seaside meadow'
Marlow	this Old English name means 'driftwood'
Marion	the meaning of this one isn't certain but can mean: 'sea of sorrow', 'rebellion' or 'wished-for child' and is a cute nonbinary name of French origin
Marquise	this is a French baby name meaning 'royalty' or a 'royal title' (ranking below duke but above an earl)'
Mason	this was originally an occupational name meaning 'one who works with stone' and is of English origin

NAME	OROGIN AND MEANS
Mckenna	is a Scottish baby name meaning 'born of fire' or 'heir of the handsome one' or 'son of Kenneth'
Mckinley	is a unique unisex name of Irish origin meaning 'son of the white warrior'
Memphis	is a unique unisex name of Irish origin meaning 'son of the white warrior'
Mercer	this French baby name means 'merchant'
Merrick	this cute gender neutral name is of Welsh origin and means 'fame', 'power' , or 'rule'
Micah	this name means 'who is like God?' and is of Hebrew origin
Mickie	this name means 'Who is like God?" it's usually the female version of names like Micheal and is of Hebrew origin
Milan	can mean 'gracious, dear' (Slavic origin), 'from the middle of the plain' (Latin origin), or 'union, coming together (Sanskrit origin)
Monahan	this unique gender neutral name is of Irish origin and means 'descendent of the little monk'
Monet	is a unique non-binary name of French origin meaning 'to be heard'
Montana	this Latin baby name means 'mountain'
Morgan	this one is such a classic androgynous baby name and means 'sea born' or 'sea song' and is of Welsh origin
Munroe	this Latin baby name means 'from the red marsh'
Murphy	this cute name is of Irish origin and means 'sea warrior'
Nash	this short and cute English name means 'by the ash tree'
Nellie	this cute baby name means 'horn', 'sunlight' 'shining light' or 'beautiful woman' and is of English origin
Nevada	this non binary name of Spanish origin means 'covered in snow' and is of Latin origin
Nico	is an Italian baby name with Greek roots meaning 'victory of the people'

NAME	OROGIN AND MEANS
Nikkie	this Greek baby name means 'victory of the people'
Noble	is an uncommon virtue baby name of Latin origin meaning 'aristocratic'
Noel	this beautiful French nonbinary name means 'Christmas' and is often given to babies born in winter
Nolan	is a cute name of Irish origin meaning 'champion' or 'descendent of the famous one'
North	this unconventional baby name suits a boy or girl and refers to the direction or pays homage to the 'North star'
Nova	is a cool name of Latin origin meaning 'new'
Oak	is another tree inspired baby name, meaning 'oak tree' which often symbolizes strength and solidity
Oakley	this Old English name is a place name meaning 'oak tree'
Ocean	this hippie baby name has become popular with crunchie moms and means a body of water-the sea
Oleander	is a cute baby name of Greek origin meaning 'evergreen tree'
Ollie	this short and cute name is of Latin origin and means 'olive tree' or 'elf warrior' (English origin)
Ombre	is a French name that means 'a color with a shaded tone or varying tones' or 'shade, shadow'
Onyx	is a gemstone name of Greek origin meaning 'nail, claw'. It refers to a beautiful black gemstone.
Orion	is a unique name of Greek origin meaning 'mountain dweller' and refers to a hunter in Greek mythology
Owen	this Welsh baby name means 'young warrior' or 'well born'
Page	this adorable name comes from Medieval culture and means attendant or 'young servant'- think Knight in training
Palmer	is a cute name of English origin meaning 'he who holds the palm' or 'pilgrim'
Paris	this beautiful name refers to the French capital of France and is perfect for boys or girls

NAME	OROGIN AND MEANS
Parker	this one is of Old English origin and is a cute nonbinary name that means 'park keeper
Patton	is an Old English name that means 'fighter's town'
Payton	this English name means 'fighting man's estate'
Pax	this name has Latin origins and means 'peaceful'
Perrie	this cute French gender-neutral badass name baby name means 'pear tree'
Phoenix	this name has a few different meanings- the common one is the legendary bird of the same name but its Greek meaning is 'dark red'
Piper	another adorable unisex baby name- this one means 'flute or pipe player'
Poe	this cute and short name is of English origin and means 'peacock'
Poet	if you're looking for a hippie bohemian unisex name, this cute English name is perfect and means ' one who writes verses'
Porter	is a unique and cute French baby name that means 'gatekeeper'
Presley	this cute English name means 'dweller at church'
Psalm	is an English baby name with Latin and Greek roots that means 'song' or 'to pluck' or 'high praise' (Hebrew origin)
Quinn	this Gaelic baby name means 'council'
Quincy	is a name of Old French origin meaning 'estate of the fifth son'
Quill	is an uncommon English name meaning 'plume' or 'feather'
Quillan	is a rare name of Irish origin meaning 'cub'
Quinlan	this is another Irish baby name and it means 'fit, shapely, strong'
Radley	is an Old English name meaning 'meadow of reeds'

NAME	OROGIN AND MEANS
Raleigh	this gender fluid baby name means 'roe deer's meadow' and is of Old English origin
Ramsay	this Old English name means 'garlic island'
Ranger	is such a cute and unique choice and is of French origin and means 'forest protector' or 'forest guardian'
Ray	this cute name means 'wise protector' and is of English origin
Reagan	this adorable Irish baby name means 'little ruler'
Rebel	is a unique English name meaning 'defiant or resistant person'
Reef	if you're looking for an ocean-inspired name, this is a unique choice. This English name means 'ridge or shoal of rock or coral near the surface of the ocean'
Reese	this classic English baby name means 'ardent or fiery'
Reign	this one is a very popular non-gendered baby name and means 'to rule' or 'sovereign'
Remington	is an Old English surname that's become a popular first name and means 'place on a riverbank' or 'raven settlement'
Rene	is a 4 letter nonbinary name of French origin meaning 'rebirth'
Renley	this unique and uncommon baby name means 'created name'
Rhodes	is a cute and uncommon non binary name of German origin meaning 'where the roses grow'
Rickie	is a classic Old German name meaning "powerful leader' or 'peaceful ruler'
Ridley	is an Old English name that means 'reed meadow'
Riley	this popular contemporary unisex name has Irish origins and means 'courageous' or 'rye clearing'
Rio	is a short name of Spanish origin that means 'river'
Ripley	is a rare Old English baby name meaning 'shouting man's meadow'

NAME	OROGIN AND MEANS
River	this Boho nature-inspired baby name means just that- river-river bank or riverside and is of English origin
Robin	this cute Old English name means 'famed, bright, shining'
Rome	is a cute Hebrew name of Latin origin meaning 'strong, powerful' or 'from Rome'
Ronnie	is a baby name of Old Norse and Hebrew origin meaning 'mountain of strength' or 'counsel rule'
Rory	this is another Gilmore Girl favorite of mine and it means 'red king' and is of Irish origin
Roslin	has multiple meanings and origins including" 'rose' (Latin origin), 'little red head' (Scottish origin), or 'gentle horse' (Old German origin)
Roux	this French baby name means 'auburn haired'
Royal	if you've got a majestic little one, this could be a cute modern choice. This English name means 'of the king/queen'
Rowan	this adorable Scottish name means 'little redhead'
Rudelle	this unique and uncommon German baby name means 'famous'
Rudi	is a short unisex name of Old German origin meaning 'famous wolf'
Rue	is a 3 letter non binary name of English origin meaning 'herb' or 'regret'
Rumi	is an adorable Japanese name that means 'beauty and flow'
Ryder	this unique nonbinary name means 'cavalryman' or ' messenger'
Ryan	is a classic baby name of Irish origin meaning 'little king'
Sage	is a cool nature inspired name of English origin meaning 'wise' or 'healthy'
Salem	is a cute gender neutral name of Hebrew origin meaning 'peace'
Sam	this Hebrew name means 'God is heard'

NAME	OROGIN AND MEANS
Samar	this name of Arabic origin means 'reward' or 'fruit of paradise' and can be used for boys or girls
Sasha	this is a Russian name meaning 'defending men'
Saylor	is such a cute nautical themed baby name of German origin meaning 'boat worker'
Sean	is a short and cute Irish name of Hebrew origin meaning 'gift from God' or "God is gracious'
Seath	is a cute and unique name of Irish and Scottish origin meaning 'wolfish'
Shay	this Gaelic baby name means 'admirable'
Shaine	this cute name with the alternate spellings means 'God is gracious' or 'beautiful' and is of Hebrew and Irish origin
Shannon	is a classic Irish name meaning 'old and wise'
Shiloh	this is another Hebrew name and it means 'peace'
Shore	is a cute Ameican beachy name that refers to the 'sea shore'
Simone	is a lovely French name of Hebrew origin meaning 'hear or listen'
Skylar	this cute English name means 'noble scholar' or 'sky'
Sloan(e)	this uncommon Irish baby name means 'little raider' or 'warrior'
Sol	this three letter nonbinary name is of Hebrew and Spanish origin and means 'sun'
Somers	is a rare Old English baby name meaning 'summer'
Spencer	this old English name has become popular with parents looking for unisex names and it means 'steward' or 'administrator'
Sterling	is a baby name of English origin meaning 'genuine',' of high quality', or 'little star'
Stevie	is an English name with Greek origins meaning 'garland' or 'crown'

NAME	OROGIN AND MEANS
Story	this cute modern American baby name means 'tale'
Sunny	this sweet English baby name means 'sunshine', 'cheerful', or 'happy'
Sutton	this androgynous baby name means 'from the southern homestead' and comes from Old English
Sydney	this cute name is used to describe 'one who lives near a wide riverside meadow' or 'from the wide island' and is of English and French origin
Tanner	this is another occupational Old English name and it means 'one who works with leather'
Tatum	this Old English name can mean 'cheerful bringer of joy' or 'Tate's homestead'
Taylor	one of my favorite unisex baby names- this one means 'cutter of cloth' and is of Old English origin
Teddy	this Old English name is usually a nickname for Theodore or Theodora which means 'wealthy guardian'
Teegan	is a cute name of Irish origin meaning 'little poet' or 'attractive, beautiful'
Tennessee	is a unique name of Native American origin meaning 'meeting place' or 'winding river'
Thierry	this French baby name means 'powerful' or 'ruler of people'
Tobi/Toby	is a classic Hebrew name meaning 'God is good'
Tommie	is a name of Aramaic origin meaning 'twin'
Toni/Tony	this cute Greek name means 'priceless one'- adorable!
Tracy	is a name of Irish origin meaning 'war-like' or 'fighter'. It can also mean 'harvester' (Greek origin)
Tristen/Tristyn	is a name of French origin meaning 'tumult' or 'outcry'
True/Tru	this cute name means 'real' or 'genuine' and is of English origin
Twain	inspired by the author- this name means 'divided in two' and is of English origin

NAME	OROGIN AND MEANS
Trinity	is a biblical baby name of Latin origin referring to the Holy Trinity
Ty	is a non binary name of American origin that means 'from the land of Eoghan'
Tyler	is a cute unisex name of French origin meaning 'maker of tiles'
Uli	this German baby name can mean 'noble leader'
Umber	this name has French origins and is a color name for a shade that is an Earthy color and means 'shade'
Val	this short and sweet English baby name means 'strong'
Valen	this is another form of Val so the meaning is the same as above, 'strong' or 'powerful'
Valor	is a unique virtue baby name of Latin origin meaning 'worthiness' or 'bravery, courage'
Valentine	is a rare name of Latin origin meaning 'strong and healthy'
Vaughn	is a cute non binary name of Welsh origin meaning 'little'
Vermont	is a cute name of French origin meaning 'green mountain'
Vesper	this Latin baby name means 'evening star'
Vie	this cute French name means 'life'
Vinnie/Vinny	this cute Latin baby name means 'conqueror'
Walker	is a name that is of Old English origin and means 'fuller of cloth'
Waverly	is a whimsical sounding name of English origin meaning 'meadow of quivering aspens
Wendall	is a cute name of Old German origin meaning 'wanderer'
Wesley	this cute baby name means 'from the west meadow'

NAME	OROGIN AND MEANS
Whitley	this cute and uncommon Old English name means 'white meadow'
Whitney	is a cute more feminine nonbinary name of English origin meaning 'from the white island'
Wilder	this cute German baby name means 'hunter'
Winslow	is a cute name of Old English origin meaning 'friend's hill'
Winter	this is a popular baby name for those born in colder months. This weather name refers to the season of Winter and is of English origin
Wolf	is a strong yet cute name of German origin meaning 'wolf'
Wren	this old English name means 'little bird'
Wyatt	this English baby name can mean 'guide' 'wide' or 'wood'
Wylie	is an Old English name meaning 'clever, crafty'
Xander	this Latin name means 'defender'
Xavi	is a rare name of Basque origin meaning 'the new house' or 'bright'
Xen	this name means 'form of Buddhism' (zen)
Xhex	this name is actually an invented name from a book and in the book, it means 'beloved one
Yale/Yael	is a name of Old Welsh and English origin that means 'heights', 'upland' or 'fertile moor'
Yanis	this Hebrew baby name means 'gift from God'
York	this Old English baby name means 'boar settlement' or 'town of the wild boars'
Yves	is a baby name of French origin meaning 'yew wood'
Zephyr	this Greek name means 'west wind'

NAME	OROGIN AND MEANS
Ziggy	is a baby name of German origin meaning 'victorious protection'
Zion	is a name of Hebrew origin meaning 'highest point'
Zoe	this Greek name means 'life'
Zuri	is a baby name of Swahili origin meaning 'good, beautiful'

BOY NAMES
WITH CUTE NICKNAMES

1. Alexander (Alex) ☐
2. Benjamin (Ben) ☐
3. Caleb (Cal) ☐
4. Christopher (Chris) ☐
5. Daniel (Danny) ☐
6. David (Dave) ☐
7. Dominic (Dom) ☐
8. Elijah (Eli) ☐
9. Elliot (Ella) ☐
10. Emmett (Em) ☐
11. Finnegan (Finn) ☐
12. Gabriel (Gabe) ☐
13. Harrison (Harry) ☐
14. Henry (Hank) ☐
15. Isaac (Ike) ☐
16. Jackson (Jack) ☐
17. Jacob (Jake) ☐
18. James (Jamie) ☐

BOY NAMES
WITH CUTE NICKNAMES

19. Jason (Jase) ☐

20. Jeremiah (Jem) ☐

21. Johnathan (Jon) ☐

22. Joseph (Joey) ☐

23. Joshua (Josh) ☐

24. Julian (Jules) ☐

25. Kevin (Kev) ☐

26. Liam (Lee) ☐

27. Lincoln (Link) ☐

28. Logan (Lo) ☐

29. Lucas (Luke) ☐

30. Maximilian (Max) ☐

31. Michael (Mikey) ☐

32. Nathaniel (Nate) ☐

33. Nicholas (Nick) ☐

34. Noah (Noe) ☐

35. Oliver (Ollie) ☐

36. Owen (O) ☐

BOY NAMES
WITH CUTE NICKNAMES

37. Parker (Park) ☐

38. Patrick (Pat) ☐

39. Peter (Pete) ☐

40. Phillip (Phil) ☐

41. Quentin (Quin) ☐

42. Richard (Richie) ☐

43. Robert (Robbie) ☐

44. Samuel (Sam) ☐

45. Sebastian (Seb) ☐

46. Simon (Si) ☐

47. Solomon (Sol) ☐

48. Stephen (Stevie) ☐

49. Theodore (Theo) ☐

50. Thomas (Tommy) ☐

51. Tobias (Toby) ☐

52. Tyler (Ty) ☐

53. Victor (Vic) ☐

54. Vincent (Vinnie) ☐

BOY NAMES
WITH CUTE NICKNAMES

55. William (Will) ☐

56. Wyatt (W) ☐

57. Xavier (Xave) ☐

58. Zachary (Zach) ☐

59. Aiden (Aide) ☐

60. Andrew (Andy) ☐

61. Anthony (Tony) ☐

62. Arthur (Art) ☐

63. Ashton (Ash) ☐

64. Austin (Aussie) ☐

65. Brandon (Bran) ☐

66. Calvin (Calv) ☐

67. Cameron (Cam) ☐

68. Chase (Chas) ☐

69. Christian (Chris) ☐

70. Clayton (Clay) ☐

71. Colton (Colt) ☐

72. Cooper (Coop) ☐

BOY NAMES
WITH CUTE NICKNAMES

73. Darian (Dari) ☐

74. Declan (Deck) ☐

75. Derek (Dex) ☐

76. Donovan (Don) ☐

77. Dustin (Dusty) ☐

78. Dylan (Dill) ☐

79. Elijah (Eli) ☐

80. Eric (Rick) ☐

81. Ethan (Eth) ☐

82. Everett (Rhett) ☐

83. Felix (Feli) ☐

84. Frank (Frankie) ☐

85. George (Georgie) ☐

86. Graham (Gram) ☐

87. Gregory (Greg) ☐

88. Harrison (Harry) ☐

89. Hudson (Hud) ☐

90. Ian (Ia) ☐

BOY NAMES
WITH CUTE NICKNAMES

91. Isaiah (Izzy) ☐

92. Ivan (Ivo) ☐

93. Jack (Jax) ☐

94. Jasper (Jazz) ☐

95. Jeremiah (Jere) ☐

96. Jonas (Jo) ☐

97. Jordan (Jordy) ☐

98. Jovan (Jove) ☐

99. Justin (Jus) ☐

100. Kaden (Kade) ☐

GIRL NAMES
WITH CUTE NICKNAMES

1. Abigail - Abby ☐
2. Alexandria - Alex ☐
3. Alice - Ali ☐
4. Amelia - Amy ☐
5. Annabelle - Annie ☐
6. Arianna - Ari ☐
7. Audrey - Audie ☐
8. Ava - Avie ☐
9. Beatrice - Bea ☐
10. Bianca - Bia ☐
11. Bridget - Bridie ☐
12. Brooklyn - Brooke ☐
13. Camilla - Cami ☐
14. Caroline - Carrie ☐
15. Charlotte - Charlie ☐
16. Chloe - Cloe ☐
17. Clara - Clarie ☐
18. Daisy - Daisie ☐

GIRL NAMES
WITH CUTE NICKNAMES

19. Daniella - Dani ☐
20. Delilah - Dee ☐
21. Eden - Edie ☐
22. Eleanor - Ellie ☐
23. Eliza - Lizzy ☐
24. Elizabeth - Lizzie ☐
25. Ella - Ellie ☐
26. Emilia - Emmy ☐
27. Emily - Em ☐
28. Emma - Em ☐
29. Esmeralda - Esme ☐
30. Esther - Essie ☐
31. Evelyn - Evie ☐
32. Felicity - Flick ☐
33. Gabriella - Gabby ☐
34. Genevieve - Genny ☐
35. Gwendolyn - Gwen ☐
36. Harper - Hap ☐

GIRL NAMES
WITH CUTE NICKNAMES

37. Hazel - Haze ☐

38. Isabella - Izzy ☐

39. Isabelle - Izzy ☐

40. Ivy - Ives ☐

41. Jacqueline - Jackie ☐

42. Jocelyn - Joss ☐

43. Josephine - Josie ☐

44. Julia - Jules ☐

45. Juliana - Julie ☐

46. Juliette - Jules ☐

47. Kaitlyn - Katie ☐

48. Katherine - Katie ☐

49. Kayla - Kay ☐

50. Kendall - Ken ☐

51. Kimberly - Kimmy ☐

52. Lillian - Lily ☐

53. Lily - Lils ☐

54. Lola - Lolo ☐

GIRL NAMES
WITH CUTE NICKNAMES

55. Lorelei - Lori ☐

56. Lucille - Lucy ☐

57. Lydia - Lyd ☐

58. Madeline - Maddie ☐

59. Madison - Maddy ☐

60. Maggie - Mags ☐

61. Makayla - Kayla ☐

62. Margot - Mar ☐

63. Matilda - Tilly ☐

64. Meredith - Meri ☐

65. Mia - Mimi ☐

66. Mila - Milie ☐

67. Natalie - Nat ☐

68. Natasha - Tasha ☐

69. Noelle - Nellie ☐

70. Olivia - Liv ☐

71. Penelope - Penny ☐

72. Piper - Pips ☐

GIRL NAMES
WITH CUTE NICKNAMES

73. Rachel - Rach ☐

74. Rebecca - Becky ☐

75. Rose - Rosie ☐

76. Ruby - Rubes ☐

77. Sadie - Sade ☐

78. Samantha - Sam ☐

79. Sarah - Sari ☐

80. Savannah - Savy ☐

81. Scarlett - Scar ☐

82. Seraphina - Sera ☐

83. Sofia - Sofie ☐

84. Sophia - Sophie ☐

85. Stella - Stellie ☐

86. Sydney - Syd ☐

87. Tessa - Tess ☐

88. Valentina - Vale ☐

89. Victoria - Vicky ☐

90. Violet - Vio ☐

GIRL NAMES
WITH CUTE NICKNAMES

91. Vivian - Vivi ☐

92. Whitney - Whit ☐

93. Willow - Will ☐

94. Winter - Winnie ☐

95. Ximena - Xime ☐

96. Yasmine - Yas ☐

97. Zoey - Zee ☐

98. Zara - Zari ☐

99. Zuri - Z ☐

100. Zoe - Zo ☐

OLD-FASHIONED BOY BABY NAMES

1. Albert ☐
2. Alfred ☐
3. Ambrose ☐
4. Amos ☐
5. Archibald ☐
6. Arthur ☐
7. Augustus ☐
8. Bartholomew ☐
9. Benedict ☐
10. Benjamin ☐
11. Bernard ☐
12. Caleb ☐
13. Calvin ☐
14. Charles ☐
15. Chester ☐
16. Clarence ☐
17. Claude ☐
18. Clement ☐

OLD-FASHIONED BOY BABY NAMES

19. Clifford ☐

20. Cornelius ☐

21. Cyril ☐

22. Daniel ☐

23. David ☐

24. Delbert ☐

25. Donald ☐

26. Edgar ☐

27. Edmund ☐

28. Edward ☐

29. Edwin ☐

30. Elias ☐

31. Eliot ☐

32. Elmer ☐

33. Elwood ☐

34. Emery ☐

35. Ernest ☐

36. Eugene ☐

OLD-FASHIONED BOY BABY NAMES

37. Everett ☐

38. Ferdinand ☐

39. Floyd ☐

40. Franklin ☐

41. Frederick ☐

42. Gabriel ☐

43. George ☐

44. Gilbert ☐

45. Gordon ☐

46. Grover ☐

47. Harold ☐

48. Harvey ☐

49. Henry ☐

50. Herbert ☐

51. Herman ☐

52. Homer ☐

53. Horace ☐

54. Howard ☐

OLD-FASHIONED BOY BABY NAMES

55. Irving ☐

56. Isaac ☐

57. Isidore ☐

58. Jacob ☐

59. James ☐

60. Jasper ☐

61. Jeremiah ☐

62. Jesse ☐

63. Joel ☐

64. John ☐

65. Jonas ☐

66. Joseph ☐

67. Joshua ☐

68. Julian ☐

69. Kenneth ☐

70. Lafayette ☐

71. Lawrence ☐

72. Leander ☐

OLD-FASHIONED BOY BABY NAMES

73. Leonard ☐

74. Leroy ☐

75. Leslie ☐

76. Levi ☐

77. Lionel ☐

78. Louis ☐

79. Lucian ☐

80. Luther ☐

81. Marcus ☐

82. Marshall ☐

83. Martin ☐

84. Maurice ☐

85. Melvin ☐

86. Merle ☐

87. Milford ☐

88. Monroe ☐

89. Morris ☐

90. Nathan ☐

OLD-FASHIONED BOY BABY NAMES

91. Nathaniel ☐

92. Nelson ☐

93. Noel ☐

94. Norman ☐

95. Oliver ☐

96. Oscar ☐

97. Owen ☐

98. Percy ☐

99. Perry ☐

100. Philip ☐

OLD-FASHIONED GIRL BABY NAMES

1. Abigail ☐
2. Adelaide ☐
3. Agatha ☐
4. Agnes ☐
5. Alice ☐
6. Alma ☐
7. Amalia ☐
8. Annabelle ☐
9. Arlene ☐
10. Beatrice ☐
11. Beatrix ☐
12. Bernadette ☐
13. Bernice ☐
14. Bessie ☐
15. Bettie ☐
16. Blanche ☐
17. Camilla ☐
18. Caroline ☐

OLD-FASHIONED GIRL BABY NAMES

19. Cecelia ☐
20. Cecilia ☐
21. Clara ☐
22. Clarice ☐
23. Constance ☐
24. Cordelia ☐
25. Cornelia ☐
26. Daisy ☐
27. Daphne ☐
28. Della ☐
29. Delphine ☐
30. Dolores ☐
31. Doris ☐
32. Edith ☐
33. Edna ☐
34. Effie ☐
35. Eleanor ☐
36. Eliza ☐

OLD-FASHIONED GIRL BABY NAMES

37. Elizabeth ☐

38. Ellen ☐

39. Eloise ☐

40. Elsie ☐

41. Emilia ☐

42. Emily ☐

43. Emma ☐

44. Enid ☐

45. Estelle ☐

46. Esther ☐

47. Ethel ☐

48. Eudora ☐

49. Eunice ☐

50. Evelyn ☐

51. Faye ☐

52. Felicity ☐

53. Flora ☐

54. Florence ☐

OLD-FASHIONED GIRL BABY NAMES

55. Frances ☐

56. Genevieve ☐

57. Gertrude ☐

58. Gwendolyn ☐

59. Harriet ☐

60. Hattie ☐

61. Hazel ☐

62. Helen ☐

63. Henrietta ☐

64. Hester ☐

65. Hilda ☐

66. Ida ☐

67. Imogen ☐

68. Irene ☐

69. Iris ☐

70. Isadora ☐

71. Ivy ☐

72. Jacqueline ☐

OLD-FASHIONED GIRL BABY NAMES

73. Jane ☐

74. Janice ☐

75. Josephine ☐

76. Judith ☐

77. Julia ☐

78. June ☐

79. Lavinia ☐

80. Leona ☐

81. Lila ☐

82. Lillian ☐

83. Loretta ☐

84. Louise ☐

85. Lucinda ☐

86. Lydia ☐

87. Mabel ☐

88. Madeline ☐

89. Mae ☐

90. Margaret ☐

OLD-FASHIONED GIRL BABY NAMES

91. Marjorie ☐

92. Martha ☐

93. Mary ☐

94. Matilda ☐

95. Maude ☐

96. Mildred ☐

97. Minerva ☐

98. Myrtle ☐

99. Nellie ☐

100. Olive ☐

UNCOMMON BOY BABY NAMES:

1. Axl ☐
2. Brecken ☐
3. Callahan ☐
4. Dashiell ☐
5. Eamon ☐
6. Finley ☐
7. Galen ☐
8. Hadrian ☐
9. Idris ☐
10. Jairus ☐
11. Kael ☐
12. Lysander ☐
13. Marcellus ☐
14. Nerys ☐
15. Oren ☐
16. Peregrine ☐
17. Quinlan ☐
18. Ronan ☐

UNCOMMON BOY BABY NAMES:

19. Silas ☐

20. Thayer ☐

21. Ulysses ☐

22. Vaughan ☐

23. Whitaker ☐

24. Xander ☐

25. Yannick ☐

26. Zephyr ☐

27. Adriel ☐

28. Bowen ☐

29. Cassius ☐

30. Darian ☐

31. Eben ☐

32. Flint ☐

33. Gideon ☐

34. Harlan ☐

35. Inigo ☐

36. Jericho ☐

UNCOMMON BOY BABY NAMES:

37. Kian ☐
38. Leif ☐
39. Maddox ☐
40. Nehemiah ☐
41. Orion ☐
42. Phoenix ☐
43. Quincy ☐
44. Rafferty ☐
45. Soren ☐
46. Tiberius ☐
47. Uriah ☐
48. Vance ☐
49. Wilder ☐
50. Xavian ☐
51. Yahir ☐
52. Zaden ☐
53. Ansel ☐
54. Beckett ☐

UNCOMMON BOY BABY NAMES:

55. Callum ☐
56. Dante ☐
57. Ellis ☐
58. Finnegan ☐
59. Granger ☐
60. Hendrix ☐
61. Ivo ☐
62. Jethro ☐
63. Kairos ☐
64. Lachlan ☐
65. Matthias ☐
66. Nico ☐
67. Orson ☐
68. Percival ☐
69. Quillan ☐
70. Rylan ☐
71. Stellan ☐
72. Tate ☐

UNCOMMON BOY BABY NAMES:

73. Uriel ☐

74. Valor ☐

75. Wolfgang ☐

76. Xavion ☐

77. York ☐

78. Zain ☐

79. Atlas ☐

80. Bastian ☐

81. Cato ☐

82. Darian ☐

83. Evander ☐

84. Fox ☐

85. Greyson ☐

86. Huxley ☐

87. Ignacio ☐

88. Jaxon ☐

89. Koda ☐

90. Landon ☐

UNCOMMON BOY BABY NAMES:

91. Micah ☐

92. Noam ☐

93. Osiris ☐

94. Pike ☐

95. Quinn ☐

96. Ryder ☐

97. Silvio ☐

98. Titan ☐

99. Ulrich ☐

100. Vance ☐

UNCOMMON GIRL BABY NAMES

1. Adalira ☐
2. Adelpha ☐
3. Aiko ☐
4. Airlia ☐
5. Alastrina ☐
6. Alcyone ☐
7. Alder ☐
8. Alecto ☐
9. Alizeh ☐
10. Althea ☐
11. Amaliah ☐
12. Amarante ☐
13. Amarantha ☐
14. Amoret ☐
15. Amorette ☐
16. Anaelle ☐
17. Andromache ☐
18. Anjali ☐

UNCOMMON GIRL BABY NAMES

19. Antigone ☐
20. Aradia ☐
21. Arantxa ☐
22. Araxie ☐
23. Ariza ☐
24. Aroa ☐
25. Asherah ☐
26. Atara ☐
27. Atheria ☐
28. Auber ☐
29. Aurembiaix ☐
30. Avonlea ☐
31. Axiom ☐
32. Azalea ☐
33. Azha ☐
34. Azura ☐
35. Baela ☐
36. Bellona ☐

UNCOMMON GIRL BABY NAMES

37. Betony ☐

38. Bronte ☐

39. Calantha ☐

40. Calypso ☐

41. Camari ☐

42. Candelaria ☐

43. Caprice ☐

44. Celandine ☐

45. Cerelia ☐

46. Chantilly ☐

47. Charmaine ☐

48. Chione ☐

49. Christabel ☐

50. Circe ☐

51. Clarimond ☐

52. Clea ☐

53. Clelia ☐

54. Coraline ☐

UNCOMMON GIRL BABY NAMES

55. Corinthea ☐
56. Cybele ☐
57. Dagny ☐
58. Damaris ☐
59. Danique ☐
60. Dariana ☐
61. Delilah ☐
62. Demelza ☐
63. Devika ☐
64. Diantha ☐
65. Dorothea ☐
66. Drusilla ☐
67. Eirlys ☐
68. Eira ☐
69. Elara ☐
70. Elspeth ☐
71. Elysande ☐
72. Embla ☐

UNCOMMON GIRL BABY NAMES

73. Endellion ☐

74. Enid ☐

75. Eowyn ☐

76. Eponine ☐

77. Eurydice ☐

78. Evelina ☐

79. Fable ☐

80. Fleurine ☐

81. Galatea ☐

82. Genevra ☐

83. Ginevra ☐

84. Halcyon ☐

85. Iridessa ☐

86. Isadora ☐

87. Isolde ☐

88. Jovienne ☐

89. Julep ☐

90. Kalinda ☐

UNCOMMON
GIRL BABY NAMES

91. Kaida ☐

92. Kalliope ☐

93. Katriel ☐

94. Kestrel ☐

95. Kiana ☐

96. Kiran ☐

97. Liora ☐

98. Lorelai ☐

99. Lumina ☐

100. Zephyrine ☐

TWIN BOY NAMES

1. Alexander and Benjamin ☐
2. Aaron and Adam ☐
3. Caleb and Connor ☐
4. Dylan and Devin ☐
5. Elijah and Isaiah ☐
6. Ethan and Evan ☐
7. Finn and Flynn ☐
8. Gabriel and Nathaniel ☐
9. Harrison and Jackson ☐
10. Isaac and Isaiah ☐
11. Jacob and Joshua ☐
12. James and John ☐
13. Jason and Justin ☐
14. Julian and Adrian ☐
15. Kevin and Kyle ☐
16. Liam and Logan ☐
17. Lucas and Logan ☐
18. Marcus and Max ☐

TWIN
BOY NAMES

19. Michael and Matthew ☐

20. Nicholas and Nathaniel ☐

21. Noah and Nathan ☐

22. Oliver and Owen ☐

23. Patrick and Peter ☐

24. Riley and Ryan ☐

25. Samuel and Simon ☐

26. Sebastian and Julian ☐

27. Theodore and Timothy ☐

28. Tristan and Tyler ☐

29. Victor and Vincent ☐

30. William and Wyatt ☐

TWIN
GIRL NAMES

1. Abigail and Amelia ☐

2. Addison and Avery ☐

3. Bella and Grace ☐

4. Brooklyn and Madison ☐

5. Caroline and Charlotte ☐

6. Chloe and Claire ☐

7. Elizabeth and Isabella ☐

8. Ella and Emma ☐

9. Emily and Eva ☐

10. Faith and Hope ☐

11. Gabriella and Isabella ☐

12. Gianna and Sophia ☐

13. Hailey and Hannah ☐

14. Harper and Haven ☐

15. Isabelle and Olivia ☐

16. Jade and Jada ☐

17. Jasmine and Juliette ☐

18. Jocelyn and Josie ☐

TWIN
GIRL NAMES

19. Kennedy and Kendall ☐
20. Lila and Lily ☐
21. Mackenzie and Madison ☐
22. Maya and Mia ☐
23. Natalie and Nicole ☐
24. Nora and Nova ☐
25. Penelope and Persephone ☐
26. Rachel and Rebecca ☐
27. Rose and Lily ☐
28. Sadie and Sophie ☐
29. Savannah and Sierra ☐
30. Stella and Sienna ☐

TOP CHOICES

Baby Names Chosen By Mummy:

TOP CHOICES

Baby Names Chosen By Daddy:

TOP CHOICES

Baby Names Chosen By O'thers:

_____
_____
_____
_____
_____
_____
_____
_____
_____
_____
_____
_____
_____
_____
_____
_____
_____
_____
_____
_____
_____
_____
_____
_____
_____
_____
_____
_____
_____

Printed in Great Britain
by Amazon

22656719R10053